Could Johnny Build a Bridge?

The deliberate dumbing down of America's kids

Du Bois/Farrar
A Fierce Ink, LLC publication

Fierce Ink, LLC
P.O. Box 128395
Nashville, TN 37212
Fierce Ink is a trademark of Fierce Music and Media

Written, designed, and compiled by DuBois/Farrar
Manufactured in the United States of America

For
Gage, Gabby,
Aidan, Chloé,
Hudson, Christian,
and
every child in
America.
May you
always
be inspired to
soar with your strengths.

CONTENTS

This book is dedicated to
John Taylor Gatto.
His body of work as
a teacher and a writer
inspires us.
His willingness to look at our book
encouraged us.
His kind message of support
humbles us.
Thank you, John, for letting us
call you "friend."

INTRODUCTION

When we first heard of Common Core State Standards (CCSS), the concept and the name sounded reasonable, even good. The sales pitch was that the governors across America were in on the development, and that states were free to "sign on or not," so ... what could go wrong, right? That's what many of us were thinking.

But the truth began to emerge, and people started asking questions. This program wasn't what anyone expected, or wanted for our children. We didn't sign up for this.

First, let us be clear: we never planned to write a book. We're mothers with careers and families, we have children and grandchildren; the children in our families attend school. These past few years we've watched our kids' attitudes toward school plummet and their homework loads grow to the point of being unbearable. These kids used to love school! Now they don't want to go.

We started researching, reading, talking to people who know what's happening. The deeper we dug, the more there was to learn. One day we looked at each other and said, how does anybody navigate all this? That's the moment we decided to collect the info, and put this book together. Our goal is to create a resource that will quickly bring you up to speed. We hope to empower you with factual information about what's happening, how to stay informed, and steps you can take to protect your children. So, fasten your seatbelt; here goes. Remember these names:

·   Arne Duncan, now former head of the DOE;
·   Michelle Rhee, a self serving promoter of CCSS;
·   Bill Gates, whose fingerprints, money and influence are all over the controls of this deleterious movement, one which now includes dedicated efforts to capture charter schools;
·   Gates' Achieve, Inc., and The Gates Foundation; these organizations have poured in many millions of dollars in influence; Gates is poised and determined to capture control of our children, whom he regards as 'human capital';

·   Pearson Publishing, the central publisher of CCSS textbooks and testing materials. Pearson brags that they possess the largest data collection of any company in the world.

·   Check the Appendix starting on page 68. We've listed many resources that offer a bigger picture of what's happening, including who these people and companies are, and how they're at the 'core' of The Common Core State Standards (CCSS). You can dig deep, or read the 'cliff notes;' either way, we hope the information here helps you feel more confident and informed about what's happening every day in classrooms across America.

The standards were not written by governors or teachers. They were written behind closed doors by noneducators, then copyrighted so they could not be changed. This process took five months, and the "secret sixty" members who participated were paid a total of fifty million dollars.

http://blogs.edweek.org/teachers/living-in-dialogue/2009/07/national_standards_process_ign.html

You may have heard about a "Validation Committee." This committee of twentynine members was ostensibly created to review, critique, and approve the standards. In this book are the names of the five members of the committee who refused to sign off on the CCSS. Their statements of objections and concerns were scrubbed from the final Committee report. But we've found some of their statements, and we've included links where you can read them.

Money was a *big* factor in getting states to 'buy in' to CCSS. And timing is everything; many states took the huge CCSS financial carrot during a very depressed economy. Now virtually all states are working to extract themselves either wholly or in part from the problematic "standards."

We mentioned Pearson Publishing (UK). Pearson is making billions of dollars from the contracts they have with American education. And it doesn't stop there.

Pearson's involvement with our children from K through 12 is profoundly invasive. Some of that includes: Pearson's software grades student essays, tracks student behavior in ways you can't imagine, and is set up to diagnose - and recommend modes of treatment for - attention deficit disorder.

This 'harvesting' is called a 'cradle to grave' collection of student data. It covers many things that have nothing to do with education and extends to information regarding the student's family. This adds alarm to our frustration over the actual classroom activities. In short, the entire movement is a federal government overreach using education as the method of entry; many are calling it child abuse.

We live in an amazing country. In this country, every child has a right to feel good about themselves; to be inspired and excited about learning. Public education, paid for with our tax dollars, should not cause any child to feel demoralized, or to dread school. But that is exactly what CCSS is producing. And as more subjects are added, it's only getting worse.

We've focused this book on math in the elementary grades - the basic standards of "'ciphering" that provide young children with the foundational tools necessary to later comprehend more complex process-based numbers concepts.

We've included examples of the types of problems our children face, with pages where you can "give it a shot" yourself. We think it tells a little bit about why our kids are stressed, unhappy, and demoralized. And frankly, we would be too.

People in rural areas, in towns, cities, and states all over America are waking up to the undeniable fact: it's time for families and communities to take back, in full measure, authority over the education of our children.

Their futures depend on it. And so do the bridges Johnny builds.

Cece DuBois & Jillian Farrar

Could Johnny
Build a Bridge?

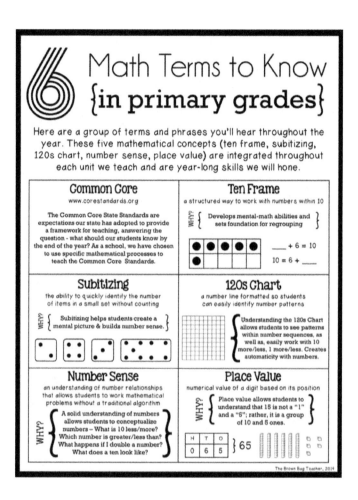

"Education is the most powerful weapon which you can use to change the world."
- Nelson Mandela

Ed note: the assignment is to find an answer that is "reasonable." There is no mention of finding the answer that is "accurate."

Find the sum. Use front-end estimation to check that each answer is reasonable.

Example

Find 354 + 291.

354 + 291 = __645__

354   +   291
↓   ↓
__300__ + __200__ = __500__

The estimated sum is __500__.

The answer __645__ is reasonable.

"Mathematics is like oxygen. If it is there, you do not notice it. If it would not be there, you realize that you cannot do without."
- Lex Schrijver

Jack used the number line below to solve 4<u>27</u> – 316. Find his error. Then write a letter to Jack telling him what he did right, and what he should do to fix his mistake.

$$\begin{array}{r} 427 \\ -\,316 \\ \hline 111 \end{array}$$

Dear __Jack_____,

   Don't feel bad. I have a Bachelor of Science Degree in Electronics Engineering which included extensive study in differential equations and other higher math applications. Even I cannot explain the Common Core Mathematics approach, nor get the answer correct. In the real world, Simplification is valued over complication. Therefore,

$$\begin{array}{r} 427 \\ -\,316 \\ \hline 111 \end{array}$$

The answer is solved in under 5 seconds — 111. The process used is ridiculous and would result in termination if used.

Sincerely,
__Frustrated Parent__

Give it a shot!

"If you end up getting something like this just
abort the mission! Abort the mission!
It is known students have died
trying to solve this."
-Anon

Second grade math ... "friendly numbers."

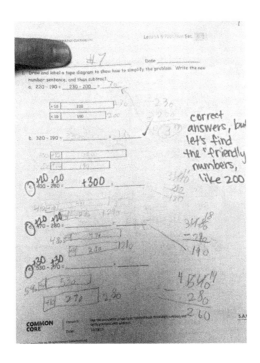

"A **friendly number** is a **number** that is a member of a **friendly** pair or a higher-order **friendly** ntuple (no, this is not a typo). **Numbers** that are not **friendly** are said to be solitary. There are some **numbers** that can easily be proved to be solitary, but the status of **numbers** 10, 14, 15, 20, and many others remains unknown." (*Hickerson 2002*)

0 + 1 =	1 + 1 =	2 + 1 =
3 + 1 =	4 + 1 =	5 + 1 =
6 + 1 =	7 + 1 =	8 + 1 =
9 + 1 =	10 + 1 =	11 + 1 =

"These integrations come
with a health warning."
- Highschool Math Teacher

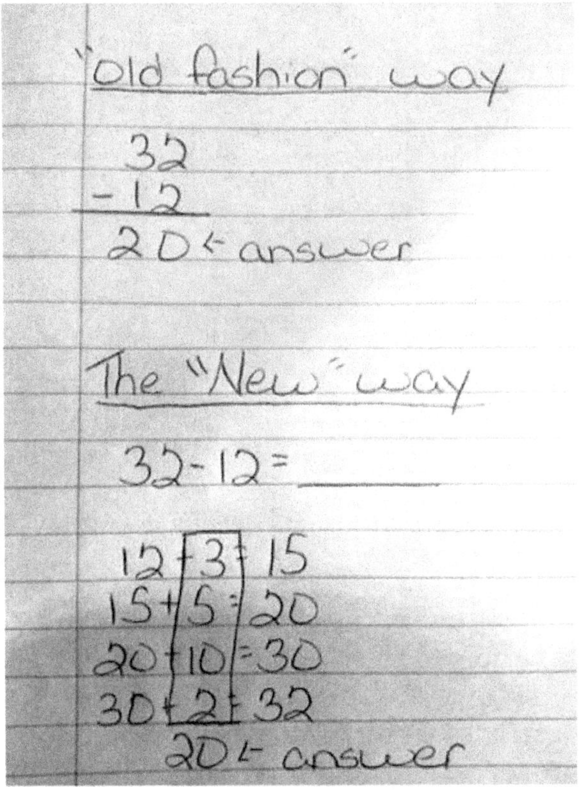

"old fashion" way

32
−12
20 ← answer

The "New" way

32−12 = _____

12 + 3 = 15
15 + 5 = 20
20 + 10 = 30
30 + 2 = 32
      20 ← answer

"There will always be people who think that you must be able to solve problems in multiple ways. This is probably similar to thinking that it is important to teach creativity in mathematics in elementary school, as if such a thing were possible.

"Forget creativity; the truly rare student is the one who can solve straightforward problems in a straightforward way."
- Dr. W. Stephen Wilson, professor of mathematics, Johns Hopkins University

Extended Constructed Response

F C R

Directions: Examine the chart and answer the questions accordingly. (*Hint: Use the strategy... In order to..... I know.....So I.... The answer is...*)

- It costs the Youth Sports Center $250 to rent each 48 –person bus. If they hire enough buses to take all the people signed up for basketball to a local tournament, **how many buses will they need to take every person? How much do they spend on buses?**

Program	Number of Participants
Basketball	128
Soccer	142
Swimming	95
Tennis	48
Weight Lifting	18

48⟌128

$250
3
$750

3 buses $750

In order to keep my job at the Youth Sports Center I know that my boss will care less about my ability to explain how to solve the problem and more about the actual correct answer. So I used real-world mathematical equations to efficiently come up with an exact answer instead of wasting valuable company time writing about the process. The answer is 3 buses and $750

Common Core DOES NOT make children college or career ready.

PARCC test items DO NOT reflect real life experiences

"If you don't think craziness will result (from CC math),
then you're being fundamentally naive."
- James Milgram,
mathematician for Stanford University

First grade math test.
It appears to be an effort to make the visuals as confusing as possible.

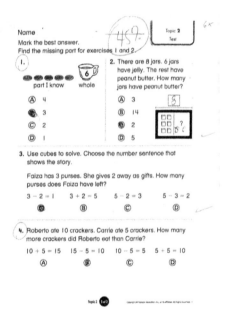

Name

Mark the best answer.

Find the missing part for exercises 1 and 2.

Topic 2
Test

1.

part I know   whole

Ⓐ 4

Ⓑ 3

Ⓒ 2

Ⓓ 1

2. There are 8 jars. 6 jars have jelly. The rest have peanut butter. How many jars have peanut butter?

Ⓐ 3

Ⓑ 14

Ⓒ 2

Ⓓ 5

3. Use cubes to solve. Choose the number sentence that shows the story.

Faiza has 3 purses. She gives 2 away as gifts. How many purses does Faiza have left?

$3 - 2 = 1$ $3 + 2 = 5$ $5 - 2 = 3$ $5 - 3 = 2$

Ⓐ   Ⓑ   Ⓒ   Ⓓ

4. Roberto ate 10 crackers. Carrie ate 5 crackers. How many more crackers did Roberto eat than Carrie?

$10 + 5 = 15$ $15 - 5 = 10$ $10 - 5 = 5$ $5 + 5 = 10$

Ⓐ   Ⓑ   Ⓒ   Ⓓ

12

"If you can't explain it simply, you don't understand it well enough."- Albert Einstein

Ed note: Starting with an easily solvable problem, New York takes the simple "7+7" and complicates it with something called "number bonds."

Name _____   Date _____

1. Use number bonds to help you skip-count by seven by making ten or adding to the ones.

(a) 7 + 7 = __10__ + __4__ = _____

       3   4

Give it a shot!

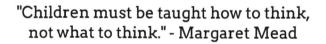
"Children must be taught how to think,
not what to think." - Margaret Mead

THIS IS MATH

$$1\ {}^1\!3$$
$$\cancel{2}4\cancel{3}$$
$$-\ 87$$
$$\overline{156}$$

THIS IS MATH ON COMMON CORE

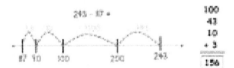

```
243 - 87 =          100
                     43
                     10
                    + 3
                    ─────
                     156
```

ANY QUESTIONS?

16

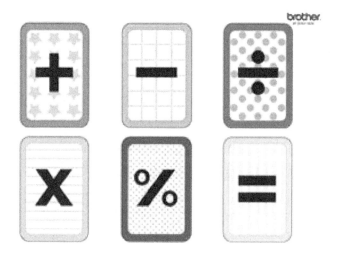

"The task of the modern educator is not to cut down jungles, but to irrigate deserts." - C.S. Lewis

Math Situation	Evidence and how to solve:
There were 21 tests on the table. The teacher (placed 16 more) on the table. How many tests are on the table?	$21 + 16 =$ → evidence of increasing ⊕ $20 + 1$ $10 + 6$ $\overline{}$ $30 + 7 = 37$ tests total
There were 24 eggs waiting to be cooked. 12 of them fell on the floor and (broke.) How many were left?	$24 - 12 =$ evidence of decreasing ⊖ $20 + 4$ $- 10 + 2$ $\overline{}$ $10 + 2 = 12$ eggs left
The teacher had 17 non-fiction books in the library bin. She also had 32 fiction books there. How many (more) fiction books did she have (than non-fiction?)	evidence of comparing Ⓒ $= 15$ more $\overset{10}{\frown}\overset{5}{\frown}$ ←——|——|——|——→ fiction 17 27 32 books (N.F.) (F.)

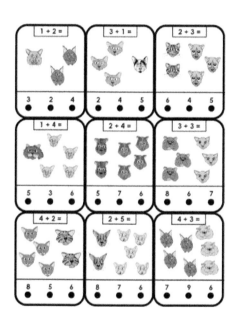

"[Kids] don't remember what you try to teach them.
They remember what you are."
- Jim Henson, *It's Not Easy Being Green:
And Other Things to Consider*

What happens when an addition problem "regroups"?

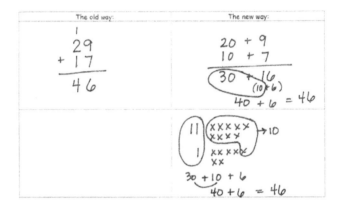

The old way:	The new way:

Q: What does evidence mean in reading?

A: We use the word "evidence" in reading a lot. We tell students to find the evidence in the text that shows you the character is mean. Or, we tell them to find the evidence in the text to show that the boy did solve his problem and found his missing dog.

Q: What does evidence mean in math ?

A: We use the same word in math to help students find the evidence in the text that shows this math situation is increasing (adding), decreasing (subtracting) or comparing (finding the amount that is different: more or less)

See examples on the back

Give it a shot!

"Do not train a child to learn by force or harshness; but direct them to it by what amuses their minds, so that you may be better able to discover with accuracy the peculiar bent of the genius of each." - Plato

The "New Way"

243
- 87

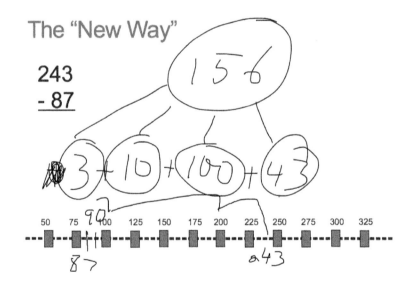

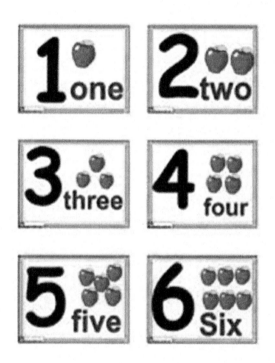

"The whole educational and professional training system is a very elaborate filter, which just weeds out people who are too independent, and who think for themselves, and who don't know how to be submissive, and so on -- because they're dysfunctional to the institutions." - Noam Chomsky

Ed note: It appears the correct answer of $33.64 is not an option.

7 Adam saved the money shown below.

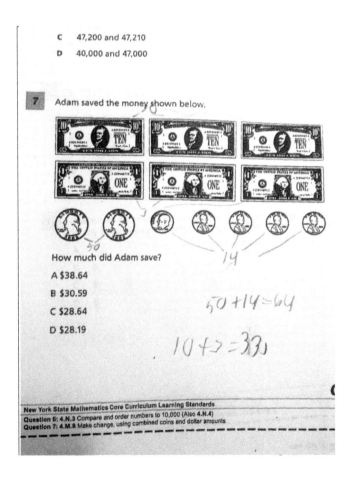

How much did Adam save?

A $38.64

B $30.59

C $28.64

D $28.19

50 + 14 = 64

10 + 2 = 33

New York State Mathematics Core Curriculum Learning Standards

Question 6: 4.N.3 Compare and order numbers to 10,000 (Also 4.N.4)
Question 7: 4.M.8 Make change, using combined coins and dollar amounts

24

one   **two**

three   **four**

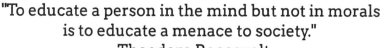

"To educate a person in the mind but not in morals
is to educate a menace to society."
- Theodore Roosevelt

A second way...

base ten block symbols:

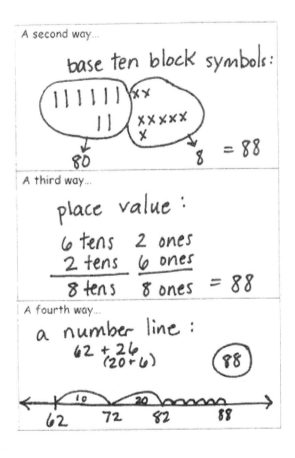

| | | | | | xx
    | | xxxxx
        x

80   8   = 88

A third way...

place value :

6 tens   2 ones
2 tens   6 ones
------
8 tens   8 ones   = 88

A fourth way...

a number line :

62 + 26
(20 + 6)   (88)

62   72   82   88
    10   20

"It is the supreme art of the teacher to awaken joy in creative expression and knowledge." -- Albert Einstein

In many classrooms, rulers are not allowed. Children are told to measure with erasers, pencils, or crayons. This is called "relative" or "approximate" measurement, as opposed to the "exact" or "finite" measurement a ruler provides. In graphics classes college professors will find it necessary to teach their students how to use, and read, a ruler. Would that be classified as "remedial ruler reading?" Wow.

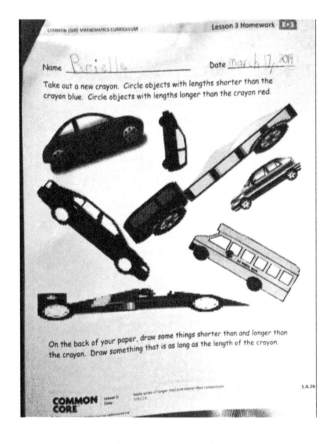

Note to future engineers: Bridges will now be measured by "CRAYONS."

Give it a shot!

"The test of a good teacher is not how many questions he can ask his pupils that they will answer readily, but how many questions he inspires them to ask him which he finds it hard to answer." - Alice Wellington Rollins

Ed note:
"Deeper understanding" = unnecessarily
complicated/convoluted, compelling
the student to:
1: Feel increasingly bad about him or herself;
2: Begin to incorporate negative self talk, like,
"I can't do it."
3: Give up
::MISSION ACCOMPLISHED::

Dear Parents,   10-1-12

We wanted to send you a "Common Core – Parent Cheat Sheet" to help you understand the processes in which your child is solving problems in math class. Remember, the philosophy of the Common Core standards is to create a deeper understanding of numbers and their values to help build a foundation for future math skills. The idea is not to just "do it" but to know "how and why" we do it. Please let either of us know if you have any questions as we are both working together with all of our students to help meet their specific needs.

Mrs.

Old Language	New Language
word problem	math situation
carry the one	regroup ten ones as a ten
borrow	take a ten and regroup it as ten ones
*add	increase
*subtract	decrease
*more than / fewer than	compare
How do you know?	evidence

Please note that we do still use "add/subtract/more than,less than", but we interchange it with the new language you see listed beside each of these words to create a deeper understanding.

The old way to solve an addition problem:	The new way to solve an addition math situation:
$\begin{array}{r} 62 \\ + 26 \\ \hline 88 \end{array}$	One way: expanded form: $\begin{array}{r} 60 + 2 \\ 20 + 6 \\ \hline 80 + 8 \ = 88 \end{array}$

"Everybody is a genius.
But if you judge a fish
by its ability to climb a tree,
it will live its whole life
believing that it is stupid."
- Albert Einstein

"Give me four years to teach the children and the
seed I have sown will never be uprooted."

-- Vladimir Lenin

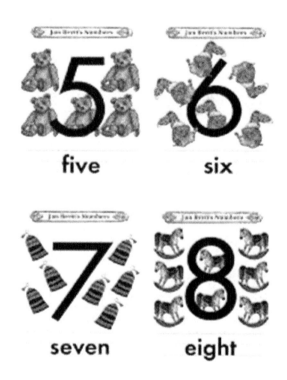

five   six

seven   eight

"If you can't explain it to a six year old, you don't understand it yourself." - Albert Einstein

Common sense trumps Common Core!

Mike saw 17 blue cars and 25 green cars at the toy store. How many cars did he see? Write a number sentence with a ▢ for the missing number. Explain how the number sentence shows the problem.

$17 + 25 = \boxed{42}$ I got the answer by talking in my brain and I agreed of the answer that my brain got.

"A teacher who is attempting to teach without inspiring the pupil with a desire to learn is hammering on cold iron." - Horace Mann

First Grade Math

Unit 2—Numbers and Operations in Base Ten

1. Fill in the missing numbers.

26, 27, 28, 29, ___, ___, ___

33, 34, ___, ___, 37, 38, 39,

40, ___, 42, 43, ___, 45, ___

47, 48, ___, ___, ___, 52, 53

2. What number is show in the set below?

_____

3. Which numeral is in the tens place in the number below?

53

○ 5
○ 3
○ 53

4. Which numeral is in the ones place in the number below?

18

○ 1
○ 8
○ 18

Write the number of tens and ones in the numbers given.

5. **60**

___ tens ___ ones

6. **14**

___ tens ___ ones

Use ___ to compare the two numbers given.

7. 42 _____ 94

8. 37 _____ 37

9. Add

23
+4

10. Find 10 more 10 less than the number given.

___ tens less **57** ___ tens more

Give it a shot!

"No man who worships education has got the best out of education. Without a gentle contempt for education no man's education is complete." - G.K. Chesterton

Fuzzy Math

The Common Core math standards serve to make simple mathematics more complicated. Here's one example of the types of "new math" many parents and teachers have been criticizing:

Add 26 + 17 by breaking apart numbers to make a ten.

Use a number that adds with the 6 in 26 to make a 10.

> Since 6 + 4 = 10, use 4.
>
> Think: 17 = 4 + 13
>
> Add 26 + 4 = 30
>
> Add 30 + 13 = 43.
>
> So, 26 + 17 = 43.

 "Nothing that is worth knowing can be taught"
- Oscar Wilde

Method A

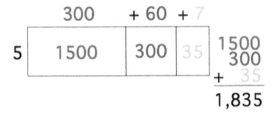

```
        300    + 60 + 7
    ┌──────────┬─────┬────┐   1500
  5 │   1500   │ 300 │ 35 │    300
    └──────────┴─────┴────┘  +  35
                             ──────
                              1,835
```

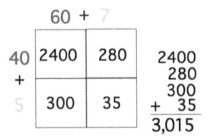

```
        60 + 7
      ┌──────┬─────┐
   40 │ 2400 │ 280 │      2400
    + ├──────┼─────┤       280
    5 │ 300  │ 35  │       300
      └──────┴─────┘    +   35
                        ──────
                         3,015
```

The **essence of mathematics**
is not to make
simple things complicated, but to
make complicated
things simple.

– Stan Gudder
Mathematician

"It is important that students bring a certain ragamuffin,
barefoot irreverence to their studies; they are not here to
worship what is known, but to question it."
- Jacob Bronowski, *The Ascent of Man*

Method B

Left to Right	Right to Left
367	367
x 5	x 5
35 5 x 7	1500 5 x 3 hundreds
300 5 x 6 tens	300 5 x 6 tens
+1500 5 x 3 hundreds	+ 35 5 x 7
1,835	1,835

Left to Right	Right to Left
67	67
x 45	x 45
2400	35
280	300
300	280
+ 35	+2400
3,015	3,015

Give it a shot!

"Imagination is the source of every form of
human achievement. And it's the one thing that
I believe we are systematically jeopardizing in the
way we educate our children and ourselves."
- Ken Robinson

Method C

7 times 5 = 35 (Decomposes into 3 tens 5 ones)
Compose 3 tens.
6 tens times 5 = 30 tens
30 tens added to 3 tens is
33 tens (Decomposes into 3 hundreds and 3 tens)
Compose 3 hundreds.
3 hundreds times 5 is 15 hundreds
15 hundreds added to 3 hundreds is
18 hundreds
(Decomposes into 1 thousand and 8 hundreds)
Compose 1 thousand.

7 x 5 = 35
(Decomposes into 3 tens 5 ones.)
6 tens x 5 = 30 tens
(Decomposes into 3 hundreds and 0 tens.)
7 x 4 tens = 28 tens
(Decomposes into 2 hundreds and 8 tens.)
6 tens x 4 tens = 24 hundreds
(Decomposes into 2 thousands and 4 hundreds

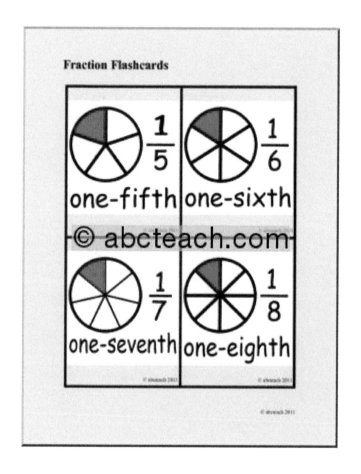

Fraction Flashcards

one-fifth | one-sixth

one-seventh | one-eighth

"Under the United States Constitution,
federal government has no authority to hold states
'accountable' for their education performance...
In the free society envisioned by the founders,
schools are held accountable to parents,
not federal bureaucrats."
- Ron Paul

Method D

$$367 \quad 300 + 60 + 7$$
$$\times\ 5$$

$$300 \times 5 = 1500$$
$$60 \times 5 = 300$$
$$7 \times 5 = 35$$
$$\overline{1{,}835}$$

$$67 = 60 + 7$$
$$\times\ 45 = 40 + 5$$

$$40 \times 60 = 2400$$
$$40 \times 7 = 280$$
$$5 \times 60 = 300$$
$$5 \times 7 = 35$$
$$\overline{3{,}015}$$

"Play is the highest form of research." -
Albert Einstein

```
46)3129
   -2300  | 50    This is half of 100 x 46
    829
   - 460  | 10
    369
   - 230  |  5    This is half of 10 x 46
    139
   -  92  |  2    Doubling is easy
     47
   -  46  |  1
     R 1  | 68
```

Give it a shot!

"The advancement and diffusion of knowledge is the only guardian of true liberty." - James Madison

$$28 \times 16$$
$$(20 + 8) \times (10 + 6)$$

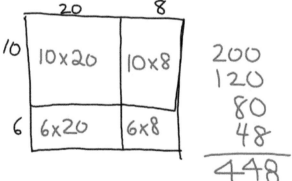

	20	8
10	10×20	10×8
6	6×20	6×8

200
120
80
48
___
448

"Imagination is more important than knowledge. For knowledge is limited to all we now know and understand, while imagination embraces the entire world, and all there ever will be to know and understand." – Albert Einstein

$$243 - 87 = 156$$

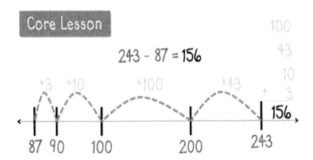

Give it a shot!

"Bodily exercise, when compulsory, does no harm to the body;
but knowledge which is acquired under compulsion
obtains no hold on the mind."
- Plato, *The Republic*

Simple Math Problem?

* Here is what my child had to do with this problem next to get a 3!

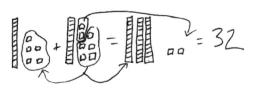

* Now to get a 4 you have to then write a sentence something like this to show you truly comprehend what it is that you are doing when you add two numbers together to get an answer.

I took five ones units from the seventeen group and added them to the other five ones units from the fifteen to make a new tens block. This gives me three tens blocks that equal thirty. The two remaining ones units from the seventeen cannot be added to anything else to make a new ten block so I added them to the tens blocks to get the answer of 32.

"What a school thinks about its library is a measure of what it feels about education." - Harold Howe

Distributive Property of Multiplication Sort

4 x 32	(4 x 30) + (4 x 2)
12 x 5	(10 x 5) + (2 x 5)
3 x 69	(3 x 60) + (3 x 9)
42 x 7	(40 x 7) + (2 x 7)
9 x 58	(9 x 50) + (9 x 8)
17 x 1	(10 x 1) + (7 x 1)

"I think you learn more if you're
laughing at the same time."
- Mary Ann Shaffer

First Grade Math
or
Teaching binaries to six year olds

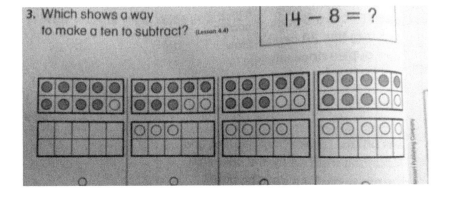

3. Which shows a way to make a ten to subtract? (Lesson 4.4)

$14 - 8 = ?$

Give it a shot!

"Liberty without Learning
is always in peril and
Learning without Liberty
is always in vain."
- John F. Kennedy

Number Bond Addition to make 10

Name:_____

6 + 8 =
6+4=10
10+4=14

Number bonds are a way for you to mentally add numbers in your head. When you think of how you can make the closest ten from the biggest number, you can create a bond. In the example, 6 is four away from 10. So you can break the 8 into two 4's. When you do that the 6 becomes 10 and what's left over is 4, so 10+4=14

8 + 7 =

6 + 5 =

7 + 6 =

9 + 5 =

7 + 4 =

8 + 3 =

5 + 7 =

9 + 6 =

4 + 7 =

6 + 9 =

7 + 8 =

6 + 7 =

Use mental math to solve.

6 + 8 =

2 + 9 =

7 + 8 =

3 + 8 =

nine

ten

eleven

twelve

"Our care of the child should be governed,
not by the desire to make him learn things,
but by the endeavor always to keep
burning within him that light
which is called intelligence."
- Maria Montessori

Clay set a goal to exercise 120 minutes each week. So far this week, he has played tennis for 23 minutes, jogged a total of 38 minutes, and swam for 42 minutes. Clay estimated that he still needs to exercise about 20 minutes this week in order to reach his goal.

How did Clay estimate?

F. $120 - (20 + 30 + 40)$

G. $120 - (20 + 40 + 40)$

H. $120 - (20 + 30 + 40)$

J. $120 - (20 + 40 + 40)$

Two friends are trying to score a total of 750 points playing a computer game. They use the equation $425 + t = 750$ to find t, the number of points still needed to reach the goal.

What is the value of t?

F. 325

G. 335

H. 1,100

J. 1,175

A student received a coupon worth c dollars off a meal at a new restaurant. The equation $12 - c = 7$ represented the cost of the meal with the coupon.

How much is the coupon worth?

A. $5

B. $7

C. $15

D. $19

Give it a shot!

"The secret of education lies in
respecting the pupil.
It is not for you to choose
what he shall know, what he shall do.
It is chosen and foreordained and
he only holds the key to his own secret."
- Ralph Waldo Emerson

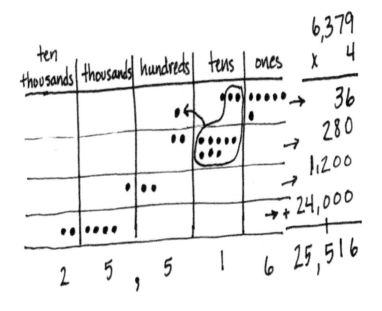

Better Than California? (Table 1) *In the Common Core, clarity can be hard to come by.*

California State Standards	Common Core
Solve problems involving division of multi-digit numbers by one-digit numbers. (Grade 4)	Find whole-number quotients and remainders with up to four-digit dividends and one-digit divisors, using strategies based on place value, the properties of operations, and/or the relationship between multiplication and division. Illustrate and explain the calculation by using equations, rectangular arrays, and/or area models. (Grade 4)
Estimate and compute the sum or difference of whole numbers and positive decimals to two places. (Grade 4)	Add, subtract, multiply, and divide decimals to hundredths, using concrete models or drawings and strategies based on place value, properties of operations, and/or the relationship between addition and subtraction; relate the strategy to a written method and explain the reasoning used. (Grade 5)
Explain different interpretations of fractions, for example, parts of a whole, parts of a set, and division of whole numbers by whole numbers; explain equivalents of fractions. (Grade 4)	Explain why a fraction a/b is equivalent to a fraction (n x a)/(n x b) by using visual fraction models, with attention to how the number and size of the parts differ even though the two fractions themselves are the same size. Use this principle to recognize and generate equivalent fractions. (Grade 4)

SOURCE: Drawn from the original standards documents by Ze'ev Wurman.

Can't Miss Videos:
You're gonna want to watch these. Seriously.

A meteorologist explains it:
https://www.youtube.com/watch?t=900&v=Tr1qee-bTZI

A student works the problem:
https://www.youtube.com/watch?t=34&v=1YLIX61o8fg

A diverse and an informed perspective on what's happening, and whats coming.
Be sure to check the video at 9:05:
"student affective sensors."
https://www.youtube.com/watch?v=d1Ubjg_o8vg

TEACHER TOM

Somewhere in the midst of our research
we stumbled upon an amazing teacher, **Teacher Tom**.
We love this guy, and we think you will, too.
Here we've included a quote from
Teacher Tom and a link to his blog.
Our goal is for every child in America to have a
Teacher Tom.

"If you don't come back here convinced that our public officials (and in particular Arne Duncan), the corporate education 'reform' movement (lead by dilettante Bill Gates and huckster Michelle Rhee), and the billion dollar industry that pushes these tests on schools (like Pearson Education, a company that earns its profits off the labor of children), are guilty of colluding to abuse young children, then I pity you. Perhaps the greatest crime is that they are succeeding in making children hate school, and by extension learning, at an even earlier age than ever. Until this year, I've never had former students return to tell me they hate kindergarten. For the first time, when parents ask for my opinion, I'm reluctant to recommend our local public school.

"It's gotten so bad, so fast that parents at the Woodland Park Cooperative Preschools are currently working on a plan to start our own kindergarten for the 2015-16 school year.

"President Obama, most recently in his State of the Union address, has made it clear that preschools are next. He seems to have bi-partisan support. I've said it before and I'll say it again, if we care about children it's now up to us to push back. We must do it for our kids and for the future of our democracy.

"This is child abuse and I'm a mandatory reporter.'"

http://teachertomsblog.blogspot.com/

" . . . a spare approach to
technology in the classroom
will
always benefit learning . . .
Teaching is a human experience.
Technology is a distraction
when we need
literacy, numeracy
and
critical thinking."

- Paul Thomas, former professor of education at
Furman University and author of 12 books on education

APPENDICES

STUDENT DATA MINING
Know your rights as parents:
Challenge the practice using existing laws

FERPA (*Family Education Rights and Privacy Act*) - Enables both parents and students to review education records and see who these records have been shared with. It offers the opportunity to have inaccuracies in the child's education corrected. If you feel your school is violating FERPA law, has denied access to your child's records (within the 45 day window), or has improperly disclosed your child's personally identifiable information, you may file a complaint.

To view the FULL FERPA LAW as recorded by the U.S. Department of Education:
http://www2.ed.gov/policy/gen/guid/fpco/ferpa/index.html

To file a FERPA complaint:
http://familypolicy.ed.gov/complaint-form

COPPA (*Childrens Online Privacy Protection*) - Does your school allow your child to use online apps, software, tests, and curriculum? If your child is under the age of 13, many of these websites and online vendors require parental consent before your child logs on.

To view the FULL COPPA LAW as recorded by the U.S. Department of Education:
https://www.ftc.gov/tips-advice/business-center/guidance/complying-coppa-frequently-asked-questions

To exercise your COPPA rights:
http://coreconcerns.weebly.com/exercise-coppa-rights/instructions-to-exercise-your-coppa-rights

To file a COPPA complaint:
https://www.ftccomplaintassistant.gov/GettingStarted#crnt

PPRA (*Protection of Pupil Rights Amendment*) - Governs the administration of surveys, analysis, or evaluation of a student under one or more of the following eight **protected areas** that pertain to the student or his/her family: political affiliation, mental or psychological analysis or concerns, sexual behavior or attitude, religion, income, privileged information, and any information that would be detrimental or demeaning to the student or family.

PPRA also concerns **marketing surveys** and other areas of student privacy, parental access to information, and the administration of certain physical examinations.

Parents have the right to inspect a survey created by a third party before the survey is administered to the child. If you feel your child has been asked these questions or had data collected without your parental consent, you may file a PPRA complaint.

To view the FULL PPRA LAW
http://familypolicy.ed.gov/faq-page/14#t14n253

To file a PPRA complaint:
http://familypolicy.ed.gov/ppra

Six Questions
Every School District Should Ask Companies, And Every Parent Should Ask School Officials, to Protect Student Data

1. What type of information does the operator collect from students?

2. Is the information used for commercial purposes? (If so, a school cannot consent on behalf of the parent.)

3. Is the information shared with third parties?

4. Are parents able to view and delete information collected from students? (If so, a school cannot consent on behalf of the parent.)

5. What security measures does the site operator take?

6. What are site operators data retention policies?

Common Core Facts
Compiled by Sandra Stotsky

1. Who developed Common Core's standards?
Three private organizations in Washington DC: the National Governors Association (NGA), the Council for Chief State School Officers (CCSSO), and Achieve, Inc.—all funded for this purpose by a fourth private organization, the Bill and Melinda Gates Foundation.

2. Who selected the members of the Standards Development Work Groups?
In the absence of official information, it seems that Achieve, Inc. and the Gates Foundation selected most of the key personnel to write the high school-level college-readiness standards.

3. Who was represented on the Standards Development Work Groups that wrote the college-readiness standards?
Chiefly test and curriculum developers from American College Testing (ACT), COllege Bound (CB), Achieve, and National Council on Economic Education (NCEE).

4. Who was not represented on the Standards Development Work Groups?
High school English and mathematics teachers, English professors, scientists, engineers, parents, state legislators, early childhood educators, and state or local school board members.

5. Are records of their meetings available?
No. These groups had no open meetings and have never provided access to any public comment or critiques they received.

6. What were the qualifications of the people selected to write the grade-level standards?
The "lead" writers for the grade-level English Language Aquisition (ELA) standards, David Coleman and Susan Pimentel, have never taught reading or English in K-12 or at the college level. Neither majored in English as undergraduates or has a doctorate in English. Neither has published serious work on K-12 curriculum and instruction. At the time, they were unknown to English and reading educators and to higher education faculty in rhetoric, speech, composition, or literary study. Two of the lead grade-level standards-writers in mathematics did have relevant academic credentials but no K-12 teaching experience. Jason Zimba was a physics professor at Bennington College at the time, while William McCallum was (and remains) a mathematics professor at the University of Arizona.

The only member of this three-person team with K-12 teaching experience, Phil Daro, had majored in English as an undergraduate; he was also on the staff of NCEE. None had ever developed K-12 mathematics standards before.

7. Who recommended these people as standards-writers, why, and how much were they paid?
The organizations that funded and developed the standards will not tell the public.

8. What was the ostensible purpose of the Validation Committee?
NGA and CCSSO created their own Validation Committee in 2009 (25 members initially) to evaluate the soundness, rigor, and validity of the standards they were developing. They have never provided a rationale for those they chose to serve on the Validation Committee.

9. Who were members of the Validation Committee?
On it were one highschool English teacher, one mathematician, no high school mathematics teachers, some testing experts and school administrators, and many mathematics educators (people with doctorates in mathematics education, or in an education school, or who work chiefly in teacher education, and who usually do NOT teach college mathematics courses). The one mathematician and the one ELA standards expert (Sandra Stotsky) on the Committee declined to sign off on the standards.

10. What was the real purpose of the Validation Committee? To have members sign a letter by the end of May 2010 asserting that the not-yet-finalized standards were (1) reflective of the core knowledge and skills in ELA and mathematics that students need in order to be college- and career-ready; (2) appropriate in terms of their level of specificity and clarity; (3) comparable to the expectations of other leading nations; and (4) informed by available research or evidence.

11. What are the chief deficiencies of Common Core's standards?
A. The standards are not internationally benchmarked. B. The standards are not research-based. C. The standards are not rigorous. They omit high school mathematics standards leading to Science, Technology, Engineering, and Mathematics (STEM) careers, stress writing over reading, reduce literary study in grades 6-12, use an unproven approach to teaching Euclidean geometry, defer completion of Algebra I to grade 9 or 10, are developmentally inappropriate in the primary grades, and use the highschool English class for informational reading instruction.

12. What reports comparing Common Core's standards with Massachusetts' standards were used to justify Massachusetts' adoption of Common Core's standards?
A. A report by Achieve, Inc. that was funded by the Gates Foundation.
B. A report by the Thomas B. Fordham Institute that was funded by the Gates Foundation.
C. A report by WestEd that was commissioned by the Massachusetts Business Alliance in Education and funded by the Gates Foundation via the James B. Hunt Institute in North Carolina.
D. Reports by Massachusetts Department of Education-appointed local/state reviewers.

13. What conclusions did these reports draw?
That there were no significant differences between Common Core's standards and the Massachusetts mathematics and ELA standards.

14. Why did Massachusetts adopt Common Core's standards in July 2010?
The state had been promised $250,000,000 in Race to the Top funds if it adopted Common Core's standards.

15. What are the major flaws in Common Core's English language arts standards?
A. Most of Common Core's reading standards are content-free skills. B. Common Core's ELA standards stress writing more than reading at every grade level. C. Common Core's writing standards are developmentally inappropriate at many grade levels and lack coordination with its reading standards. D. Common Core expects English teachers to spend at least half of their reading instructional time at every grade level on informational texts. E. Common Core reduces opportunities for students to develop critical thinking. F. Common Core's standards are not "fewer, clearer, and deeper;" they often bundle several objectives into one statement and call it one standard.

Sandra Stotsky *is Professor Emerita of Education Reform at the University of Arkansas, where she held the 21st Century Chair in Teacher Quality. She is credited with developing one of the country's strongest sets of academic standards for K-12 students as well as the strongest academic standards and licensure tests for prospective teachers while serving as Senior Associate Commissioner in the Massachusetts Department of Education from 1999-2003. She has also written several in-depth analyses of the problems in Common Core's English language arts standards. She is the author of The Death and Resurrection of a Coherent Literature Curriculum: What Secondary English Teachers Can Do (Rowman & Littlefield, June 2012).*

Resources:
Mark Bauerlein and Sandra Stotsky. (September 2012). How Common Core's ELA standards place college readiness at risk. http://pioneerinstitute.org/download/how-common-cores-ela-standards-place-college-readiness-at-risk/ R. James Milgram and Sandra Stotsky (September 2013)

Lowering the Bar: How Common Core Math Fails to Prepare High School Students for STEM. http://pioneerinstitute.org/news/lowering-the-bar-how-common-core-math-fails-to-prepare-students-for-stem/

Validation Committee members
James Milgram, Sandra Stotsky, Dylan Wiliam, Barry McGaw, and Alfinio Flores
refused to sign off on the Common Core "standards." Their concerns and objections were scrubbed from the official report.

Statement from Doctor James Milgram
https://advancingnheducation.files.wordpress.com/2014/02/written-new-hampshire-testimony.pdf

Testimony from Sandra Stotsky
http://www.uaedreform.org/downloads/2014/08/testimony-for-the-ohio-rules-and-reference-committee-on-substitute-hb-597.pdf

The "secret sixty" wrote the standards
for a total of $50,000,000.00.
It took them five months;
only one teacher among them.
Check it out.
http://blogs.edweek.org/teachers/living-in-dialogue/2009/07/national_standards_process_ign.html

::CHECK IT::

**If you review nothing else in this book, please,
take the time to watch the following
presentations
by**

Dr. Duke Pesta.

**These videos explain, better than
anything we've seen,
the government's plan to
"program"our children;
the ways in which CCSS is designed to
change how our
children view the world.**

**Learn what is
headed for our children
in the classroom.**

What Dr. Pesta shares here is important.

Knowledge is power.
Watch them.

https://www.youtube.com/watch?v=7Odvein76aw

https://www.youtube.com/watch?v=-htDV60CjkA

Cradle to Grave Data Harvesting and Tracking
of
Every Child
in
America

One of the many violations being inflicted on all students as a result of Common Core standards and Common Core tests is the massive increase in database monitoring of students from "cradle to grave."

On June 9, 2009, Arne Duncan, then U.S. Secretary of Education, gave a speech in which he explained why he wants to use Common Core tests and standards to track student data from the cradle to the grave:

*"We need robust data systems to track student achievement and teacher effectiveness. We want to see more states build comprehensive systems that track students from pre-K through college and then link school data to workforce data. We want to know whether **Johnny** participated in an early learning program and completed college on time and whether those things have any bearing on his earnings as an adult."*

Ed. note: The information Duncan "wants to see/wants to know" about Johnny is not, and never has been, the government's business -- in fact, any thinking person knows the idea is a blatant, illegal invasion of privacy. But the aggressive proponents of such a movement are end running the Rule of Law by very careful "wordsmithing." Pay close attention.

Duncan's full speech:
http://www2.ed.gov/news/speeches/2009/06/06082009.html

Important information:
http://michellemalkin.com/2014/10/09/
look-whos-data-mining-your-toddlers/

CCSS TERMS TO REMEMBER:

"Data Mining" - The collecting from our children of personal, family, political, religious, financial, and environtmental information through testing, surveys, observation, computer games, sensory readers, and other techniques for the purposes of profiling, identifying, categorizing, and classifying our children and our families. Did your child have an emotional upset or meltdown at school that school officials called you about? Ask to see his file. Chances are good that it's in there permanently.

"Data Exhaust" - The trail of digital cookies or "tags" left by our children, including but not limited to their work, interaction, responses to teachers or fellow students; when they answer questions about anything, play games, when they respond or fail to respond to any stimulus be it emotional, oral, written, or digital. All of this information is recorded, harvested, and algorythms are created that pertain specifically to each child. Furthermore, the government has complete access to the entire record of every schoolaged minor in the country; they have the authority to share it with whomever they choose, "as long as the wording is framed correctly so as to bypass privacy laws."

"360 View of the Child" - In order for The Common Core to "succeed," every single element pertaining to our children - in any way - must and will be recorded, and reported. Does my six-year-old son like macaroni and cheese but won't eat vegetables? Does my ten-year-old daughter bite her nails? Does she sleep with a stuffed animal? Do I read to my children before bed? Do my children say prayers before sleep? Do they climb in our bed when it storms? All "previously" private information will now be a part of our children's "governmental data file," and will follow them ... "from prenatal to grave."

"One Size Fits All Education" - The Common Core

is a rigid set of "standards" that leaves no room for our children to soar with their strengths. The Core approach is "teach to the test." This means our children spend their days learning how to regurgitate the right information on tests so that the schools they attend will achieve the scores necessary to qualify for government money. Our children are now considered to be government capital in a country where depth and breadth of their learning and knowledge no longer have any bearing on their classroom time. Remember Pink Floyd's song, "Another Brick in The Wall"? Yeah, well ... give it another listen. In fact, watch the video. The "normal" school day depicted in it is happening in our cities, and those are our children on that conveyer belt.

https://www.youtube.com/watch?v=YR5ApYxkU-U

"Grit, Tenacity & Perseverance" - These are

described by the CC documents as "multifaceted concepts encompassing goals, challenges, and ways of managing these. We integrate the big ideas from several related definitions in the literature to a broad, multifaceted definition of grit for the purpose of this report: "Perseverance to accomplish long-term or higher-order goals in the face of challenges and setbacks, engaging the student's psychological resources, such as their academic mindsets, effortful control, and strategies and tactics."

Ed, note:
The third video link on page 65 explains -- complete with visuals -- the "student affective sensors." Please watch it. According to plan, these will be used on our children to evaluate their "grit, tenacity and perseverence."

Reference Material

DATA MINING: CCSS

http://stopcommoncoreillinois.org/privacy-issues-data-collection-from-cradle-to-adulthood/

http://www.theamericanconservative.com/common-core-and-data-mining-fact-and-fiction-part-ii/

http://truthinamericaneducation.com/category/privacy-issues-state-longitudinal-data-systems/privacy-invasiondata-mining/

http://www.thenewamerican.com/culture/education/item/15213-data-mining-students-through-common-core

http://www.thenewamerican.com/culture/education/item/16193-orwellian-nightmare-data-mining-your-kids

http://www.thenewamerican.com/culture/education/item/16647-expert-explores-link-between-federal-data-mining-and-common-core

http://truthinamericaneducation.com/privacy-issues-state-longitudinal-data-systems/common-core-data-collection/

OBJECTIONS GROW, TRUTH REVEALED: CCSS

http://weaponsofmassdeception.org/2-common-core-fake-standards/2-4-support-for-common-core-plunges

http://www.breitbart.com/big-government/2016/01/21/exclusive-former-pearson-exec-reveals-anti-american-agenda-in-common-core-on-constitution-guns-christianity/

http://www.thenewamerican.com/culture/education/item/16192-common-core-a-scheme-to-rewrite-education

http://www.thenewamerican.com/reviews/books/item/19664-common-ground-on-common-core-book-demolishes-common-core-fraud

http://www.thenewamerican.com/culture/education/item/18170-as-common-core-becomes-punchline-critics-win-battles-nationwide

http://www.huffingtonpost.com/peter-greene/common-core-standards_b_5346907.html

http://www.corestandards.org/Math/Content/mathematics-glossary/glossary/

Reference Material

http://www.corestandards.org/assets/commonCoreReport_6.10.pdf

http://www.thenewamerican.com/culture/education/item/16627-strategies-to-defeat-common-core-education-gain-momentum

http://www.uaedreform.org/downloads/2013/11/common-cores-invalid-validation-committee.pdf

http://pioneerinstitute.org/download/claims-and-facts-about-common-core/

http://takingnote.learningmatters.tv/?p=6232

http://resoundingbooks.org/press/press-kit.pdf

TEACHERS SPEAK OUT: CCSS

http://truthinamericaneducation.com/tag/jane-robbins/

http://www.arkleg.state.ar.us/assembly/2015/Meeting%20Attachments/410/I12866/Robbins%20Common%20Core%20Data%20Collection%20Testimony.pdf

https://americanprinciplesproject.org/app-education/jane-robbins-stop-common-core-series/

http://truthinamericaneducation.com/common-core-state-standards/james-milgram-discusses-common-core-math-standards-on-fox-business/

http://nhfamiliesforeducation.org/content/letter-teachers-forced-implementing-common-core-simply-changing-name-and-collecting-student-

http://www.thenewamerican.com/culture/education/item/20443-in-resignation-oklahoma-teacher-blows-whistle-on-common-core

https://whatiscommoncore.wordpress.com/tag/james-imilgram/

http://truthinamericaneducation.com/tag/american-principles-project/

http://teachertomsblog.blogspot.com/2013/04/good-teacher-are-flaw-in-system.html

LEGITIMATE ALTERNATIVES TO SAT/ACT TESTING

https://arc.greathomeschoolconventions.com/

Heroes Among Us

We want to wrap things up by sharing with you a couple of the heroes we've discovered on our journey through the minefield of compulsory education:
John Taylor Gatto and **John Caldwell Holt**.
We're sure there are many others out there, but for us these are two individuals who shine above the rest. Please check them out; you'll be informed and inspired.
We guarantee it.

John Taylor Gatto

https://www.tragedyandhope.com/th-films/the-ultimate-history-lesson/catalog/

John Taylor Gatto comes in as our favorite, and not just because he sent us words of encouragement after seeing this book. John is a highly celebrated educator who's been on a crusade for children most of his adult life. His books lay bare the government system that indoctrinates our children in the name of education, and he offers solutions to the very real problem inherent in the institutional structure.
John Taylor Gatto is a true hero to us all.

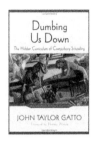  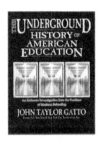

John Taylor Gatto's books are must reads for those of us who want to understand what's happening, and what we can do about it.

www.johntaylorgatto.com

http://www.amazon.com/John-Taylor-Gatto/e/
B001K7SOAE/ref=ntt_aut_sim_1_1

John Caldwell Holt

John Holt was an American author and educator, a proponent of homeschooling and, specifically, a champion for the "unschooling" approach.

http://www.johnholtgws.com/

http://www.amazon.com/John-Caldwell-Holt/e/
B000APT25Y/ref=sr_tc_2_0?qid=1457741843&sr=1-2-ent

FRONT LINE
Plug In:

Time is in short supply for all of us. So here's a list of brilliant minds, and their resources. Even if it's on the go, and one at a time, check them out. Diane, Karen, Women on the Wall (Alice Lenahan), Dr. Pesta, Tina -- all are among those literally on the "front line" for American children. They offer up to date information, and present fresh and exciting options for how we educate our children. Inform yourself, and spread the word.

Diane Ravitch
http://dianeravitch.net/

Karen Bracken
http://www.starvethebeastusa.com/

Women on the Wall
http://womenonthewall.org/

Dr. Duke Pesta
https://www.youtube.com/playlist?
list=PLWnICFNoZscgb_bvCnLxMRySQojlryH9a

Freedom Project Academy
https://www.fpeusa.org/

Tina Hollenbeck
www.hsroadmap.org

Truth in American Education
http://truthinamericaneducation.com/

Homeschool Legal Defense Organization
http://www.hslda.org/

FINAL WORDS

Listen:
We know that what we've included here is the tip
of the iceberg; the CCSS and the DOE landscape is
constantly changing. We don't pretend to have
all the answers. But in this book we've gathered
information and resources that we feel are some
of the best available.

And together we can reclaim the control and
authority of our children's education:

· Check online for like minded groups in your
area and nationally
· Look for and connect with groups on social
media sites like Facebook
· Dig deep in the **Reference Material** we've
included on pages 79 and 80
· Check the **Front Lines** links we've provided on
page 83
· Get and stay involved, refer back to this book if it
helps, and check our site for updated information
as it comes available.

www.couldjohnnybuildabridge.com

To express your concerns
regarding Common Core,
please contact the office of your governor.

http://www.nga.org/cms/home/governors/staff-
directories--contact-infor/col2-content/governors-office-
addresses-and-w.html

Resources

P. 1 An Educator's Life: August 2010

P. 2. http://www.momdot.com/common-core-is-making-me-stupider/

P. 4. http://www.theblaze.com/stories/2014/03/24/youve-just-got-to-see-what-a-frustrated-parent-wrote-on-their-childs-common-core-math-assignment/

P. 6. https://twitter.com/smheath11/status/448280845280096256/photo/1

P. 8. www. thefederalistpapers.org

P. 10. https://exceptionaldelaware.wordpress.com/category/common-core/

P. commoncorestandards.org/math

P. 12. nationalreview.com Ten Dumbest Common Core Problems

P. 14.www.stopcommoncore.com

P. 16. www.truthinamericaneducation.com

P. 18. http://www.washingtonpost.com/blogs/answer-sheet/wp/2014/11/08/why-so-many-parents-are-freaking-out-about-common-core-math/

P. 20. wtfrly.com 2+2= What? Confusing Mathematics Common Core Style

P. 22.www.pixshark.com

P. 24. www.nationalreview.com The Ten Dumbest Common Core Problems

P. 26. www.nationalreview.com The Ten Dumbest Common Core Problems

P. 27. CARTOON

P. 28. www.thetruthwins.com

P. 30. Common Core Parent Cheat Sheet

P. 32. CARTOON

P. 34. http://mrconservative.com/2014/03/37945-7-year-old-outsmarts-ridiculously-stupid-common-core-question/

P. 36. common core math first grade

P. 38. http://www.theblaze.com/blog/2014/04/29/common-core-math-standards-fuzzy-at-best/

P. 40. https://www.pinterest.com/nicoleskeene/5th-grade-math/

P. 42. https://www.pinterest.com/nicoleskeene/5th-grade-math/

P. 44. https://www.pinterest.com/nicoleskeene/5th-grade-math/

P. 46. https://www.pinterest.com/nicoleskeene/5th-grade-math/

P. 48. www. libertyunyielding.com/2014/04/01/common-core-lesson-simple-division/

P. 50. Numbers and Operations in Base Ten Grade Three

P. 52. www.wgquirk.com/mult.html

P. 54. www.nationalreview.com/.../ten-dumbest-common-core-problems

P. 56. http://www.mathgoodies.com/glossary/term.asp?term=Distributive%20Property%20%20of%20/Multiplication

P. 58. http://dailycaller.com/2014/02/08/how-bizarrely-complex-can-common-core-make-simple-arithmetic-for-americas-children/

P. 60. www.helpingwithmath.com › By Subject › Addition

P. 62. https://jeopardylabs.com/play/mct-2-math-test-review

P. 64. www.vestal.stier.org/Downloads/VH67.pdf

.

Notes

Notes

CPSIA information can be obtained
at www.ICGtesting.com
Printed in the USA
LVOW05s0450150317
527243LV00014B/28/P